FREDDY'S FOX

Anthony Masters

Illustrated by Mike Perkins

Hi, I'm Anjali. See how Freddy and I deal with the Baxter bullies and a ghost!

A & C Black • London

comix

First paperback edition 2003
First published 2002 in hardback by
A & C Black Publishers Ltd
37 Soho Square, London W1D 3QZ
www.acblack.com

Text copyright © 2002 Anthony Masters
Illustrations copyright © 2002 Mike Perkins

The rights of Anthony Masters and Mike Perkins to be identified
as author and illustrator of this work have been asserted by them in
accordance with the Copyrights, Designs and Patents Act 1988.

ISBN 0-7136-6192-5

A CIP catalogue record for this book is available from the
British Library.

A & C Black uses paper produced with elemental, chlorine-free pulp,
harvested from managed sustainable forests.

Printed and bound in Spain by G. Z. Printek, Bilbao

CHAPTER ONE

Bill and Ed Baxter were twins and not the kind of people to mess with. Freddy was horrified. How could they be so cruel? The brothers even had an admiring crowd of boys around them in the playground.

Everyone looked at Freddy in surprise. No one argued with the Baxters.

He didn't care what he said to the Baxter brothers.
He loved animals. Bill turned to Freddy.

Ed and Bill were towering over him now.

None of the other boys dared to help him. They just stood watching as the Baxters picked Freddy up and dropped him into the bin. It was full of the remains of yesterday's lunch.

The Baxters found a fox's den in the scrapyard. They're going to kill it.

What can we do?

See if we can find that fox first.

CHAPTER TWO

Freddy and Anjali were nervous as they arrived at the scrapyard on the edge of town, but there was no sign of the Baxters.

In the middle of the yard stood the crushing machine and a huge crane which soared right up to the sky. There were piles of old cars on one side of the machine and flattened cars on the other.

Then, from behind one of the piles, Bill Baxter stood up.

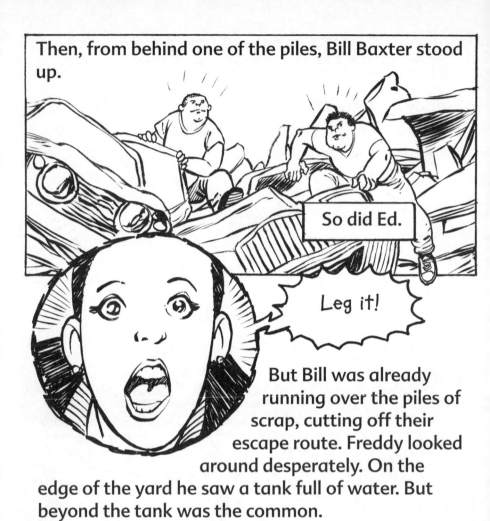

So did Ed.

Leg it!

But Bill was already running over the piles of scrap, cutting off their escape route. Freddy looked around desperately. On the edge of the yard he saw a tank full of water. But beyond the tank was the common.

He began to run. So did Anjali, but Bill and Ed ran faster and cut them off again.

Bill grabbed Freddy and Ed took hold of Anjali. Just then, there was a shout from a caravan on the opposite side of the yard.

The man was big and burly and there were tattoos all over his arms.

The Baxter brothers began to run.

Anjali and Freddy went in the opposite direction.

CHAPTER THREE

Freddy was walking home from school on his own when he saw the fox. He was lying on his side under some bushes by the roadside and his paw was cut and bleeding. As Freddy crouched down beside him, he saw the fear in the animal's eyes.

Don't worry, I'm not going to hurt you.

Freddy put out his hand, hoping to stroke the fox's head. But it drew its lips back in a snarl.

Freddy wasn't afraid. He felt good when he was with animals and planned to be a vet like his uncle when he grew up. He suddenly grabbed the fox and picked him up. For a moment the fox struggled and then stopped.

The fox's breath was coming in short, sharp gasps and he was trembling all over.

With the fox in his arms, Freddy began to run for home.

But suddenly he paused. Maybe taking him home wasn't such a good idea after all. His parents would be bound to phone the vet for help and maybe his fox would get put down. He had to find somewhere else to hide him. Then Freddy had an idea.

She'd died over a year ago now, but her house was still empty.

Freddy ran down a side street and through some iron gates that led into a wilderness garden.

This place is like a jungle.

Old Mrs Butterworth's ghost was said to prowl the grounds. Feeling as scared as the fox, Freddy stumbled along an overgrown path until he came to the house. The paintwork was peeling and some of the roof had fallen in.

There was a long, low building next to the house.

That must have been the old stables.

A door was swinging open. Freddy stopped, shivering. In his arms the fox shivered too. Inside, the stables were dark and musty. Freddy pushed open the door of one of the loose boxes and laid the fox on the straw.

I'll be back.

Half an hour later Freddy returned with a torch and a first aid kit. Freddy had also managed to bring an opened tin of dog food, a bowl and some water. Freddy went over to the fox and crouched down beside him.

Gently he took the paw and, using some cotton wool, began to clean the wound and bathe it with antiseptic. Then he bandaged the paw carefully.

Freddy was amazed to find the fox didn't struggle this time.

CHAPTER FOUR

Freddy came back the next morning and was relieved to find that not only had the dog food been eaten, but the fox was sleeping peacefully.

Reassured, Freddy ran all the way to school, catching up with Anjali on the way. He told her about the fox and what he had done.

Come back and see him after school.

What about the ghost of Mrs Butterworth?

What about her?

She's meant to be prowling round without her head.

I didn't see her.

Despite her fears, Anjali joined Freddy in the wilderness garden after school.

The fox was still lying on the old straw. He looked up at them fearfully.

As Freddy took off the bandage and bathed the fox's paw with antiseptic again, Anjali peered outside.

There's something moving.

Freddy got up and joined her. Swollen rain clouds had gathered outside and thunder was rumbling somewhere in the distance.

Where?

At the window

Anjali was staring at the old house.

There's nothing there.

You're looking at the wrong window.

There — can't you see her?

Anjali pointed frantically.

Anjali was gazing intently at each window in turn.
Dark shadows seemed to be moving everywhere.

Anjali was not in a mood for Freddy's joking.
Suddenly, lightning lit the sky and Anjali began to run.

Freddy went back into the stables and knelt down by the fox again.

Freddy wasn't sure but he thought the fox looked a bit better. Then the fox suddenly licked his hand.

CHAPTER FIVE

The Baxter brothers looked up at their father fearfully.

They were all standing in the back yard, looking down at the loose chicken wire and what was left of the scared chickens.

Ed and Bill said nothing. They were as scared of
their father as the chickens were scared of the fox.

Mr Baxter was still furious.

CHAPTER SIX

The next morning Freddy was about to head down the path towards the stables when he found Anjali at his side. Today was Saturday and Freddy hadn't seen Anjali since last night when she had run away into the darkness.

They ran for the bushes. As they crouched in the thick foliage they heard the Baxter twins talking by the gates.

Bill sounded rather nervous.

Their voices faded away and after a while Freddy and Anjali got up.

I thought you'd be too scared of the headless woman to turn up again.

I'm here.

And I'm staying.

Anjali was indignant.

When they opened the stable door, the fox was on his feet. He went over to the bowl of dog food and started to eat.

36

I wonder why he doesn't do a runner.

It's amazing to get this close to a wild animal.

I think his paw is healing.

Freddy looked down at it.

We should put him back in the wild.

Isn't this place wild enough?

Anjali looked round fearfully.

The Baxters are bound to find him when they come back after football.

So what are we going to do?

Freddy was silent. Then he had an idea.

I've got a cat box at home. Let's go and get it.

CHAPTER SEVEN

Freddy got his bike out of the shed. He found an old strap and Anjali helped him fix the cat box to the front of the bike. Then Anjali had a brainwave.

Anjali only lived down the road and she was soon back on her own bike. She'd fixed another cat box on to the front.

Freddy gazed at his friend in admiration.

Back at the stables, Freddy picked up the fox. But now he was better he began to struggle.

Eventually, with Anjali's help, Freddy got the fox into the cat box and shut the lid tightly.

Then he and Anjali began to cycle down the weed-covered drive. Anjali kept looking over her shoulder.

What are you looking for? The headless woman?

No. The Baxters. They could be hiding in the bushes, waiting to jump us.

But there was no sign of an ambush as Anjali and Freddy pedalled towards the gates.

I think we're in the clear.

Then they saw the Baxter twins sitting on their bikes, waiting for them. They looked triumphant.

Freddy whispered under his breath.

> If we get split up, I'll see you back at Butterworth's.

> Okay, go for it!

Freddy cycled furiously and was soon out of sight. Anjali deliberately made a slow start so the Baxter twins would follow her and give Freddy a chance to get away. It didn't take them long to pass Anjali and skid their bikes across the road to block her.

Ed snapped open the cat box.

There's nothing inside.

You sneaky little...

Freddy's got that fox!

They turned their bikes round and began to cycle after Freddy. Now they were angry, the Baxter twins pedalled faster. Anjali watched them disappear into the distance. What was she going to do? Then she had another brainwave.

CHAPTER EIGHT

Freddy was heading for the woods. This was the proper wild, not an overgrown suburban garden. He cycled as fast as he could, his bike rocking about on the uneven path, but when he looked over his shoulder he saw the Baxters close behind. Ed was in the lead, grinning nastily.

Freddy wondered what the Baxter brothers would do if they caught him.

Legs aching, Freddy pedalled frantically. Then he saw the path led to a fast flowing stream that was bridged by a narrow plank.

Freddy rode on to the plank and began to wobble across.

Several times he thought he was going to topple over the edge into the water and drown his fox.

But somehow he managed to get across the plank and pedalled as hard as he could down the path, heading deeper into the woods.

Then he looked back again.

The Baxters were wading across the stream, their bikes over their shoulders. They weren't going to trust the plank.

I've got to release the fox, like, now!

Freddy skidded to a halt and leant his bike against a tree. He knew he only had seconds before the Baxter brothers would catch up with him.

Freddy opened the cat box and grabbed the fox, gently putting him on the ground.

The fox crouched down, looking up at him with puzzled eyes.

Freddy took the bandage from his paw.

But still the fox stared up at Freddy, puzzled, uncertain

Ed jumped off his bike, flinging it to the ground.
So did Bill and then they both began to chant.

Suddenly, Freddy's fox burst into a run, darting through the trees. Both the Baxter boys started in pursuit. But they were on foot and Freddy knew they hadn't the slightest chance of catching him.

He got back on his bike, turned round and began to pedal hard, back towards town.

Then Freddy heard a wild shout behind him and looked back.

The Baxter brothers had given up chasing the fox. Freddy breathed a sigh of relief, but it only lasted a second. Now the twins were coming after him. Desperately increasing his speed, Freddy rode over the plank without the slightest wobble this time.

The Baxters decided to risk riding over the plank too. But almost immediately they began to wobble and first Ed and then Bill fell into the stream with enormous splashes.

Slowly the Baxters struggled out. They were soaked through and covered in mud. Freddy had a head start.

Riding up Mrs Butterworth's drive as fast as he could, Freddy hoped Anjali had remembered his instruction.

But there was no time to look for her now. The Baxters were close behind him again and Freddy knew he had to hide.

He found some dense bushes just before the stable block and pushed his bike deep into the foliage. Then he crawled in too.

Freddy was only just in time. Peering through the leaves he could see the Baxters, soaked through and furious, cycling down the drive.

As Freddy lay there, trying not to move a muscle, he heard a strange wailing sound. He glanced up at the darkening afternoon sky, shivering with fear and wondering whatever the sound could be.

Suddenly, the Baxters began screaming in terror and Freddy could hear them cycling back up the drive as fast as they could.

Cautiously, Freddy stood up, and to his horror saw a figure at the second floor window which looked misty and unclear.

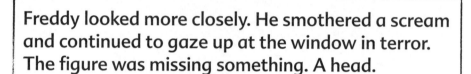

Freddy looked more closely. He smothered a scream and continued to gaze up at the window in terror. The figure was missing something. A head.

The ghost of Mrs Butterworth had come to his rescue.

Terrified, Freddy crouched down under the bush, his hands over his ears, trying to block out the eerie wailing sound.

He didn't stand up again for a long time.

When Freddy cautiously peered out, he saw Anjali running towards him, a cloth half over her head and a large shaggy mop under her arm. Suddenly, Freddy realised what Anjali had done for him. She had rigged herself up as the headless ghost of Mrs Butterworth.

As they cycled back home, Freddy knew he and Anjali would have to try and keep out of the Baxters' way for a good long while. But for the moment they didn't care.

64